My Mommy and Me

Malgosia Piatkowska   Sam Hilton

ARCTURUS

My Mommy is very special.

We do lots of fun things together.

My favorite meal is...

Mommy likes to eat..

Draw pictures of your delicious food here.

My plate

Mommy's plate

The animal I love most is

....

Mommy's best animal is

....

Draw a picture of the two animals playing together.

My number one movie is

....

Inside this wallet is a card for Mommy.
Can you make it special for her? Here are some ideas!

- Write "To Mommy" inside the card.
- Draw her a picture.
- Sign your name at the bottom.
- Add kisses by writing "X."
- Put the card inside the envelope and write her name on the front.

Give the card to Mommy
to show her how much you
love her.

Draw one of the characters from a book
that Mommy reads to you.

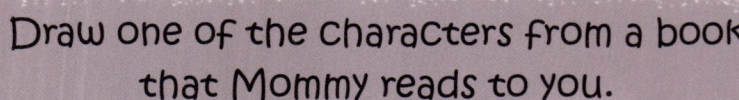

When she was little, Mommy liked to read

....

My favorite book is

....

Mommy's favorite vacation was to

....

Show you and Mommy on vacation together here.

The best place I've ever
been to on vacation is

....

Mommy likes to play

....

Draw a picture of you playing your sport here.

The sport I like to play most is

....

Mommy's best ice cream is

....

Add the toppings to these cones to show your favorite ice creams.

My favorite ice cream is ....

When Mommy was my age, her favorite toy was

....

Show your favorite toy here. Draw Mommy's too!

The toy I like best is

....

When she was my age, Mommy's best friend was named

....

You and
your
best
friend

Mommy and
her best
friend

Draw pictures, or stick some photos here.

My best friend is named

....

Think of the best bit from your favorite movie and draw it here.

If Mommy could see any movie, she would choose

....